The Dedalus Press

The Stubble Fields

Patrick Moran

The Stubble Fields

Patrick Moran

Paddy Moran

DEDALUS

The Dedalus Press
24 The Heath ~ Cypress Downs ~ Dublin 6W
Ireland

© Patrick Moran and The Dedalus Press, 2001

ISBN 1 901233 78 2 (paper)
ISBN 1 901233 79 0 (bound)

Dedalus Press books are represented and distributed in the U.S.A. and Canada by **Dufour Editions Ltd.**,
P.O. Box 7, Chester Springs, Pennsylvania 19425
in the UK by **Central Books**, 99 Wallis Road, London E9 5LN

The Dedalus Press receives financial assistance from
An Chomhairle Ealaíon, The Arts Council, Ireland.

Printed in Dublin by Johnswood Press

Contents

Artesian	9
Bird Migration	10
Ordination Sunday	11
Nuns' Cemetery	12
Cot Death	13
Terminal	14
The Giant Panda	16
Alcoholic	18
At the Daycare Centre	20
Workshop for the Handicapped	21
Origins	22
In Memoriam	24
Poker School	25
Prime Time	26
Break-Up	27
After the Crash	28
Dreamland	29
Birthplace	30
Circus	32
Spoiled Priest	33
Going Back	34
Stubble Fields, After Spraying	35
Bog Lane	36
Where?	37
The Moment	38
The Last	39

Man Dying	40
Bill	41
Faith Healer in Age	43
Patient	45
Shortcomings	46
Refugee	47
Local History	48
Achill	49
Epithalamium	50
Passing the Royal Hotel	51
Ritual	52
Birth	53
The Dark Road	55
Rough Drafts	56
Leaving Sunday Mass	57
At O'Connell's Pub	58
The Birds	60

FOR MARGARET, MARY AND JAMES

ARTESIAN

Again. Out of my father's hoard
Of stories, his brooding clouds.

Out of my mother's spirit,
Singing through its pain and fret.

Out of a soul weaned on green.
Out of the marred streams, the bird-wane.

Out of the bowed heads, raised chalice, host;
Out of the residues, the bearings lost.

Out of silences, slurred words,
The nights of starred and starless cards.

Out of pressed lips, hearts laying tracks.
Disposable couplings. Cul-de-sacs. . .

Out of it all, somehow, this welling up
To the tongue's tip, to pen-tip.

Bird Migration

The sun vestigial over shorn fields.
Inklings of chill. The evenings closing in.
Time to leave staid nests under roofs and eaves,
      To let their world take wing.

They fly past French vineyards, stately chateaux;
Over the Pyrenees; through burning plains
And Congo jungles; roosting on Zulu huts,
      Or tall oasis palms.

Their instinct is more keen than any map:
Intricacies of flight and days of rest
Are resolved in prompt return to last year's haunts
      For sun and insect-feast . . .

But what of all those killed in storms and fires?
Even the pain is part of their mystique:
Shrouded in pattern and quest, they stiffen
      To indelible beak.

ORDINATION SUNDAY

Moving among bubbly voices, bowed heads,
Their hands charged with healing and reprieve,
The new priests had the air of just-fledged birds
As they imparted blessings in solemn words.
I clutched each memento like a treasure-trove...

And, years later, it would all echo still:
Even when altars were ticking with time-bombs;
When priests seemed corseted in ritual,
And loaves and fishes were only bones and crumbs.

Nuns' Cemetery

Row after row almost identical:
Low, black railings enclosing little plots
From each of which a simple white cross sprouts
To Sister Pius, Catherine, Gabriel. . .

Clocks could have been set by those lives, those days
Learned by rote; yet no one is left to tell
What emotions ranged behind the veil,
Whose souls grew radiant, or nebulous.

But now they are at rest; those whose hearts bowed
To chastity and prayer; whose dark habits
And clacking rosaries were set for high notes.
Those whose voices broke. And those who found their God.

Cot Death

Even still, they open doors on
dolls and rattles; the empty cot;
a dress waiting for her to grow.

Laying her down was hard, but now
the least thing brings her up: beaming,
making towards them, unstoppably.

TERMINAL

Propped up in bed — your face
Flushed and haggard, traces
Of jet-black hair amid the grey —

The bulky frame had shrunken.
Your voice seizing on
The exhalations of wheezy

Breathing, emerged tiny,
Burdened with phlegm and
Protracted bouts of coughing.

But your talk was game as always:
Recalling high-pitched nights in pubs,
The vagaries of cards,

The epic local matches.
And I couldn't help thinking of
Your unobtrusive kindnesses;

How you'd make peace in arguments,
Or hush malicious gossip.
I'd often meet you

On summer evenings, your greyhounds
Straining at the leash as we
Whiled time away with chat. . .

Now, I could find no soothing words,
Only a clichéd babble
As I made my last farewell.

You faced the final days
Of running sores and sleeplessness
And tissues soaked with phlegm,

Still dreaming of lambent nurses
With armfuls of cotton wool
And the perfect soporific.

The Giant Panda

When the leading expert,
Professor Pan, was a child
And first saw the giant panda,

He was fascinated by
The snowy face, the shaded eyes;
Its lumbering gait

And shy, solitary air.
But he could not have known then
What it would entail:

Years of pleading with governments
To ease deforestation,
Using electronic collars,

Hidden cameras, camouflage
To monitor and preserve
This bamboo gourmet

Daintily, indolently
Chewing leaves and shoots;
Years learning, sifting, ordering...

As the habitats kept shrinking,
As numbers kept depleting,
His purpose becoming clearer:

To distil a life
Into pure panda, the record
Of all that he had seen,

All that might have been.

ALCOHOLIC

The muffled greeting
as he shuffles in
to his corner stool

to set out again
on a spree of beer
and double whiskies;

his random comments
on sport and weather
just a camouflage

as he lapses
into dark recesses. . .
Until he resurfaces

in the small hours: retching,
his hands trembling
to light a cigarette;

his mind re-forming
the inevitable
question: *why why why?. . .*

To compose disquiets,
salve memory's running sores?
To be delivered?

To sense intimations
of harmony somewhere
between the first flow

and the hangover?

AT THE DAYCARE CENTRE FOR HOMELESS MEN

Each day, the homeless gather here,
Bearing relics from their last squat
In bulging plastic bags.
One keeps sucking a damp-stained butt;
Beside him, a man with matted hair,
The scar on his forehead jagged.

Another is sniffing a rose
As he wistfully hums a tune.
A hunchback peruses
Crumpled tabloids, his pinstriped trousers
Tucked into wellingtons. Someone
Is shaking to the hangover blues.

But now they join the straggling queue
For steaming mugs and sustenance.
Afterwards, they play cards,
Pace the room, listen to records;
Or drift into reminiscence
Until the hours are whiled away.

A few watch racing on TV,
Obsessively: that unison
Of hands and heels; the poised
Whips; the all-out charge for the line;
And the hooves' diminuendo
When the winning-post is passed.

WORKSHOP FOR THE HANDICAPPED

Watching these painstaking fingers stumble,
or a foot that keeps slipping

off the pedal, you almost recoil
from the humps and twists and botches.

Until you note the eyes — serene, intent
as if nothing mattered

but the tireless quest for outlet
through dim passages of flesh

into the gleam of finished things:
sewing boxes made from icepop sticks;

lampshade tassels designed like bells;
tapestries stitched with singing hearts.

ORIGINS

i.m. Philip Larkin

Prickly, introspective, you might even
Have been half-content browsing through *The Magnet*
Or fantasising in your room, alone;
Or just playing with your train set.

But your parents were always bickering:
Their anger simmering against the lid,
Forever on the verge of boiling over
In your pressure cooker childhood.

Your father would emerge from tense silences
To vent imperious, airtight attitudes;
Mousy, fretful, your mum would wring her hands
Crying out his verbal raids.

Fogged up, bound, your stammer like a stigma,
You were on the run from muddle and pain. . .
Only to lurch into writing: words bursting
Mercurially from your pen.

* * *

Till you perfected your imaginary
Flights through real bars: against the costive,
Prefixed words old hungers beating still —
And flutterings of love as if

You never could forget that when your parents
First met, the air seemed to be charged with high
Romance, signs of happy-ever-aftering
Which would detonate in you.

IN MEMORIAM

His verses rarely stirred divining rods,
and never found the ease of trampolines.
yet he wore poetry like a habit.

Each night, his heart beating to word and rhyme,
he'd strain beyond grease and skins, the crushed butts,
the single bed: all for a dream of wings

that led, finally, to his own backyard. . .
his coat and glasses folded on the rim
of the dark tank they fished his body from.

Poker School

Again, they enter the smoky world
Of false scents, inspired bluffs: each bet

A high road or a cul-de-sac.
Shuffling the pack, gathering the cards,

Fingers seem bewitched by silver;
Though eyes are sphinx-like, the blinds down

Upon the pain of losing streaks,
The shivering in threadbare hands. . .

Inured to hope, they've schooled themselves
To see a new dawn in every deal:

The cards falling like pilgrim steps
Toward a cloudburst of coins, manna-rain.

Prime Time

We'd been in pubs till the small hours,
Celebrating Jim Dunne's stag night.
There was much watering of roots,
And cosy looking back on years;
And talk pushing out its boats,
And ribbing over bedsprings, bridal suite...

But what kept flashing before me
Were my wild oats and the late nights;
Itchy couplings, seedy flats ;
The card games fraught with destiny...
Always, the helpless urge to go for it —
And what had I to show for it?

On the way home, I stopped to pee.
The air was all hay and lilac,
As if summer were reaching out to me...
It was not enough — I was not enough.
I was falling through fingers, through
Hedge and grass like petals, like chaff.

BREAK-UP

We drove back through dense fog that night
After a pre-Christmas dinner dance,
(Another row, more dissonance),
Parting abruptly at your flat.

All that arduous journey, no yield,
No dovetailed talk, no saving grace;
Just the crackling of our thin ice,
Tirades and tears against lips sealed.

And I thought then of what we'd been.
The threshold-squeak of touch and kiss.
The flickerings. The fretted ease.
Splashing through waves at Killakeen.

But most I recalled our setting off —
After what seemed like breaking through,
Like stumbling into empathy —
Upon that moonlit mountain drive:

Past ripe meadows, the water's roar;
Then, up tree-lined paths, hand in hand,
As if what we were looking for
Was just around the next bend.

After the Crash

There had been so many journeys;
so much foraging for passion;
so much groping through froth and smoke

that when my car spun off the road
I could scarcely reconcile
the one who'd been a hive of dreams

with the figure struggling from the mess,
his watch still ticking through the sirens
into a dawn of shattered glass.

Dreamland

To have been here so often before,
Yet keep coming back for more;

Back to the night-club's throbbing sound,
To lights flashing DREAMLAND DREAMLAND

Into the heart's recesses,
Stirring up old flames and ashes. . .

To endure vigil and rebuff,
The hopes that wilt to a perfume whiff —

All for the prospect of release
In flowing words and charged embrace:

When risen being is so in tune
That dancefloor feels like trampoline.

Birthplace

She is growing old:
stretchmarked from years of tillage,
seeding, reaping.

Her expanded pastures
bearing scars of surgery
on vibrant hedges.

Her summer finery,
her fragrance subdued by toxic
deodorants.

In winter, shivering
in ruts, unsheltered ditches;
passing fouled waters.

Her memory is fading:
each funeral, each shut-up house
just more dead brain cells. . .

Her past is as real now
as sepia-tinted photos
of a vanished era:

birdsongs opening
on dog-rose and whitethorn;
her pristine streams,

her unshorn tresses;
the haycocks rising,
dome-like, in her aftergrass.

CIRCUS

Gaudy posters would whet our appetite
to see those nomads come and pitch their tents.
We were hooked on it all: the ring master,

imperial in dicky-bow and tails;
clowns grovelling for applause; the acrobats
swinging on trapeze far above the nets.

We'd sit agog as lions snarled at whipcrack;
as, nonchalant with parasol, a girl
walked the tightrope, step by tingling step. . .

Homing, I'd shield the spell like a nest egg:
all about me, old talk, the tents toppling,
and every wagon set to pack and vanish.

Spoiled Priest

They still recall him stealing to the pub:
black-hatted, stubble-faced, his coat badged with stains.
Stranded in silence, he'd drink the whiskey neat,
his ashen eyes kindling into embers. . .

Even when he'd gone, and chat rose again,
old talk of crops and women fizzled out —
as if there lingered in the smoky air
echoes of Angelus, a whiff of incense.

Going Back

It was here my birds first took wing,
Here where my eyes were schooled in green,
My soul raised on a vigil light.
Here were tales of rath and changeling;
Open fires; the unending lane.
All that made me articulate . . .

Now, there's a whiff of poisoned buds.
Stalwarts doddery, brittle-boned.
Houses left to sag and wither.
Rusted gates. Weeds. Skeletal sheds.
And I feel like a child who's found
His world at the end of a tether.

Stubble Fields, after Spraying

Though gripped by lingering toxic mist,
these stubble fields still keep the faith.
Birds dart from the ragged hedges.
The stumps, erect and military,
bristle against wellingtons. . .
Yet sowthistles that seem bushy,
evergreen are glazed and droopy,
the buds and leaves have shrivelled up;
while undergrowth, lately a quilt
of unobtrusive flowers and grass,
is frazzled to a rusty brown —
all those beseeching shoots and blades:
a congregation of bowed heads.

Bog Lane

Long gone the turf-cutters whose sods,
Harvested with patient hands, sleán and barrow,
Were carted home in brimming loads.

Now, despite the NO DUMPING signs,
People stealthily bring their rubbish here:
Abandoned toys, mattresses, tins.

By day, only a few — doctor,
Priest, relatives — routinely go to see
The scattered old still living there:

Sleek cars weaving between potholes
Compelled to slow to a funeral pace;
Teeth gritted against rumbling wheels. . .

Sometimes, young lovers come at night;
Leaving behind butts, beer cans and condom
Wrappings: *Gossamer, Fetherlite*.

WHERE?

Where are those do-or-die football matches?
The spun-out yarns? The camaraderie?
Where are the horse-drawn days, the airy dances?
The fraught kisses? The rolling in the hay?

In shrinking homes, wafery hospices.
In rosaried hands, and feet become arthritic.
In quaint voices that keep stumbling on
Dusty relics from some mental attic.

The Moment

Some were shuffling through a dole queue,
Or in the bookie's scanning odds;
Others were loading turf or straw.
Kitchens, offices and sheds,
Whole parishes seemed to hold their breath
When news broke of Joe Ryan's death.

Suddenly, he passed before their eyes,
Not as in the after years —
When his droll talk had lost its ease,
And so much had gone astray in bars —
But undiminished, in his prime,
The greatest player of the time.

Again, they felt those epic games
Build up: flags, expectant crowds;
The pipe bands leading out the teams;
The match releasing them like gods . . .
Games that so often peaked with Joe
Coaxing the ball into his sway;

Or emerging out of the ruck,
Opponents lunging in his wake;
Or poised to score a stunning goal. . .
Until memory fell through the trapdoor
Of all that was so vivid still —
But now was no more.

AT LAST

She had grown so precarious
her mind was like a boat
that kept bumping off reason's banks;
her words a fumbling for matches
when the lights go out.

Stock-still there amid all she'd known:
her well-used *Lives of the Saints*;
spools and patterns, "work in progress";
the prizes won at shows;
flower beds choked with weeds, matted grass. . .

A world slipping through outstretched hands.
A voice mustering
old days, and loved ones underground.
A huddle of memories
making a last stand.

Man Dying

Had you no idea? Though you faced
A glut of pills, months of exhaustive tests;
The nausea, the loss of appetite —
Often puking up the bit you'd eat —
You dismissed it as just a stubborn flu,
A caller in no rush to go.

On those mellow September afternoons,
You'd stroll down the familiar fields and lanes
As surprised, as gratified as anyone
With the cloudless skies, unseasonal sun;
The farmers still out working in their shirtsleeves,
Hardly a sign of withering leaves.

Sometimes, wisps of straw you'd see on hedges,
Or sods of turf fallen into ditches
Would recall your working life: sowing the seeds,
Tending cattle; callused hands, reaping blades. . .
Did you, remembering the harvests past,
Ever think this might be your last?

People kept telling you how well you looked.
(Though many guessed how frail you were, how racked.)
Up to the very end, you went to Mass
And cheered at matches; played cards, drank your glass.
And you were still there, pushing open doors
When death took you, unawares.

BILL

Often, in the fading light,
The quiet unleafing,
I'd meet him shuffling home;

Ready as ever
To relive his dancing nights:
The rhythms piercing him;

The to-and-froing press
Between the sets; old flames
That lit up his being . . .

His itchy yearning flaring
In breaking words;
The bare uncurtained eyes.

*

When they released him
From the mental hospital,
He had to face the music:

Bleatings, lowings, birds rising
From the greening hedges . . .
Until, unbearably,

Women shimmied before him
Like a June meadow
To the mower's hum.

*

The last time I met him,
He'd been homing late from work
With a dodgy torch,

When he suddenly stalled:
Afraid of losing footing
On the icy road.

So I helped him — the ribs
Of spirit showing through
His mumbled, sheepish thanks —

Down the hill, bidding goodnight
As he opened the door,
Fumbled for a light.

Faith Healer in Age

With her high-boned, sunken. cheeks
And straggly hair, she might be
Just another ageing spinster,

Were it not for her nunnish eyes;
Her hands so meekly joined;
And, despite her welcoming me,

The way her chat keeps lapsing
As if she were retreating
To an inner sanctum.

Now, only the shrinking old
Are left to testify
To the cures she wrought.

There's no anthology
Of *before* and *after*
Photos to show how skin

Was cleared of ringworm's
Hideous, spreading lesions;
Shingles, rashes, eczema.

There are no tabloid headlines
To storm indifference,
To blare out *Miracle*!

Nor am I still the boy
Who came here years ago
To be cured of tetters;

Who wondered, meeting her,
If she lived on morsels,
Sacrificed sleep for prayer;

The boy who, in the dim light,
Watched her removing relics
From their satin cases

Before applying them
To the diseased flesh
In a trance of litanies;

Who wriggled in her gaze;
Who felt like fleeing, but
Stayed rooted to the spot.

PATIENT

Her rose-embossed, heart-shaped tin,
emptied of its gift sweets,
is now the repository

for a bewilderment of pills
which rest on her outstretched tongue
as lightly as the Communion host.

Day after day, year after year...
Through the relentless pain that makes
her crutch-bound steps a Calvary,

through the unresting, tickling nights:
her sufferings composed in prayer,
her heart delivered in its singing.

SHORTCOMINGS

For years I watched my father crouch,
Intent, among the budding crops,
Shaking the life out of hated weeds.

He'd build loads fastidiously,
Would mould the hay to tapered cocks.
Sods flew, unstraining, from his sleán.

Each evening, having milked the cows,
He'd come in, rubbing thorn-scratched hands,
His eyes set for broken weather.

At night, he'd read: turning pages
Into alluring worlds, mouthing
The big words like a neophyte.

Often I foundered on his tongue,
Yet I never stopped coming back
To seek him out beneath the gruffness...

Now, half-blind, he reads my poems
With a magnifying glass, but
Falters on the rugged lines

As if he could hear Goldsmith still,
Welling up from schoolroom dust:
Immaculate, and off by heart.

REFUGEE
>*after Ungaretti*

In the ruined streets, I beg
the small change of your souls . . .

Of these houses nothing remains
only rubble, stumps of wall.

Of so many who were close to me,
nothing is left, not even that.

But in the sanctuary of my heart
no cross is missing.

LOCAL HISTORY

In these pages, dead streams flow again.
Places wear their christening robes:
Kilclooney, Toher, Lisdaleen . . .
Churches are recalled from ruins,
The names seem clearer on the grave slabs.

ACHILL
for Margaret

Some day, maybe, I'll be able
to see it purely as it is,
without prospect or retrospect;

to see the rusting cars and tractors
as just a feature of the landscape
like the stone-walled fields, haycocks, sheep;

to walk the unpeopled roads, saying
the names without nostalgia:
Bóthar na Marbh, Bealach an Trá. . .

And see you — there, now — after a swim,
splashing out through the shallows
on the track of the setting sun.

Epithalamium

Coming from your push-button world,
Its routines of work and play:
The outings with the girls, the dates;
The free-flowing pubs and nightclubs;
(And nights comparing notes!),

What a change it must have been
To wed a man who still dug peat;
Who'd fondly rouse smoored seed at dawn
Or coax tongues of flame from embers;
A husbander of heat...

Until gradually you, too,
Would be infiltrated by fire:
Clearing ashes, bearing in sods;
At night, waiting cosily for
Heat to crackle the rads.

Passing the Royal Hotel, Tipperary Town

Instinctively, I imagine
what's going on within: raised tongues;
races being rerun;
drinkers, maybe, in wobbly flight;
or a wedding and its burgeonings;
cards dealt for a big pot. . .

But you say there's more to it than that:
the yearnings fraught with wear and tear;
skivvies clearing the mess
of dregs and fag-butts, misguided piss;
mornings after dogged by nights before;
the embers of regret.

RITUAL

The curtains drawn, the lights off:
time for us to shed again
lingering traces of restraint. . .

Watching you unfussily
assume your nightie, I lie
trigger-tense as always:

marvelling at, riveted by
the obstinate, pale scar
on your sunkissed thigh.

Birth

I
Sowing beech

I've just spent hours planting
these saplings: opening ground,
bedding the roots in a dark womb. . .

Now is the time when hopes and frets
rummage for the groove of prayer:
that shoots be not rebuffed by wind;
that the roots be given rain;
that the long vigil
culminate in budding.

II
Newborn

No acclaim which would later come —
the cards and gifts; the relatives who'd scour
memory to fit each infant feature
in the ancestral pantheon —

could match that first seeing her safe:
delivered from the dark world of failed sperm
and pregnancies which never reach full term —
there, bawling through our stunned relief!

III
Baby, Elderly Relatives

Is it because they've heard it all before —
the tales which run like railway lines;

the reminiscing about dances
and matches, the hard winters, long summers —

that their responses seem so cursory,
the nodding of heads so mechanical?

Or is it because
their minds are really on the baby?

Trying to decipher her babble,
to fathom those suddenly dilating eyes,

follow her pointing finger. . .

THE DARK ROAD

Work-bound now, I no longer bide
The town's snail-like traffic jams,
The stasis at the right of way;
Where a huge *Finches* soft drinks ad.,
Showing an empty cage, proclaims
Go on. Set your spirits free!

Instead, I go by the short cut
Popularly called The Dark Road,
Which I knew in my dancing prime
As a secluded courting spot:
Cars nosing in, gravid with dream,
To seek the dark at Knox's wood.

Now, mile by mile, through bumps and muck,
Past hard-hat men felling the trees,
I drive, more tense as school looms near:
Another day of trying keys
To Wordsworth, Yeats, Dickens, Shakespeare;
Of urging *Take up your pen and walk.*

Another day of scribbled notes;
Of raw voices; red biro ticks;
Of minds sunk in apathy.
Unbridgeable gaps. Culture shocks.
Again I face the graffitti
Makers, the stragglers through the gates.

Rough Drafts

While Piggott was a flow of hands and heels
In timing yet another winning run;
While McEnroe was disguising top-spin lobs
Or uttering passing shots down the line,

My heart in hiding stirred. I'd raise my voice
In pubs amid frothy intimacies;
And yet, at night's end, how often did I hear
My spirit beat against the drained glasses?

There were flutterings at discos, sealed lips.
At poker games, I played so recklessly
They said that I'd see God. I was swaying
Between Compostela and Thermopylae. . .

And what's left now? Nothing but rough drafts
Around which, ivy-like, amendments cluster;
The titles flickering still: *Broken Signposts,
Relics, A Poem Found in the Gutter.*

Leaving Sunday Mass

       Bowed heads, God-forming lips. . .
Out of it all, I emerge to the brood
Of tombstones sprouting in the church's shade,
       The click of heels down steps.

       At the holy water
Font, I make a cursory sign of the cross:
What was flourished once with such childlike grace
       Shrunken to a flutter.

At O'Connell's Pub

So much the same: the low-pitched talk, the smoke
Rising; each face a closed or open book;
The pool table where sinking the black ball
Once seemed for us, too, all in all;
The young still here, nursing dreams of wild oats —
Remember our dancing, women-questing nights?
And the many sessions that we spent here
Plotting a literary career?

Now you're back on holidays once more; now
Quite the man about town and raconteur,
Dismissing your old ambitions with a quip:
"Promise dies in rejection slips. . .
Do you still tend the flame?" "Oh, my poetry's
More like a torch with dodgy batteries",
I riposte, but can hardly disguise the ache
Of waiting still for the rod to shake.

Then, as always, talk drifts to families
And friends. Our kids growing beyond our ways.

Tim's blighted air. JJ split up again.
Another dying down the lane.
We ponder how sermons once corseted
With God now seem so airy, lightly clad.
How hedges, fields. . . A whole weave unravels
To JCBs, graveyard shovels.

We elegise: what else is there to do?
"Hitch a lift on the info super-highway",
You jest, "the brave new world of Internet
And Megabyte... Too late for that".
Yet nostalgia's not what it used to be:
Despite our fond rummage through memory,
The unfailing anecdotes, your high gloss,
We keep facing a sinking glass

Till closing time, till another session floats
Down an urinal clogged with fag-butts.
Outside, the young rev up, take off like birds;
While we set out with muted words
On roads fraught with bends and breathalysers.
("So much," you'd say, "for life's little pleasures".)
And I feel my whole being springing cracks,
My feet unsteady in their tracks.

The Birds

Surely they know their world is not as it was.
What sense can they make of malodorous air?
Or hedgerows cut to the quick? Or felled trees?
Even worms are risky fare.

But now, another spring is stirring: time
To build. What use is it to feel a pang
For unmolested green, a lost sublime?
All they can do is *sing   sing   sing*.